TREES

OF THE PACIFIC NORTHWEST

npedersen

Dedicated to
W. Sherman Pedersen
for his expert guidance and encouragement

TREES

OF THE PACIFIC NORTHWEST

PORTLAND GARDEN CLUB
PORTLAND, OREGON

Copyright © 1996
The Portland Garden Club
1132 S.W. Vista Ave.
Portland, OR 97205

Library of Congress Catalog Number
96-070516
ISBN 0-9639462-1-8

Printed by Premier Press
Portland, Oregon

PREFACE

Trees are one of the most valuable natural resources of the Northwest. In the past, trees were essential to the survival of the Native Americans and the early settlers. Today, the forests provide us not only with a variety of wood products, but also with clean water, with habitat for numerous wildlife species, and with some of the most beautiful scenery in the world. This book briefly describes the most common forest tree species, with common and scientific names. The charts include leaves, fruit, bark, habitat, and uses. We hope the book will spark your interest in the wonderful trees of the Pacific Northwest. Enjoy!

FRIENDSHIP IS A SHELTERING TREE

SAMUEL TAYLOR COLERIDGE

CONTENTS

TREES
CONIFERS

INCENSE-CEDAR
Calocedrus decurrens
Cypress Family   Up to 150 ft.

Incense-cedar, like Alaska cedar and western redcedar, is not a true cedar. True cedars are found only in a band from North Africa, the eastern Mediterranean, and east to the Himalayas.

WESTERN REDCEDAR
Thuja plicata
Cypress Family   Up to 175 ft.

This was the most important tree to the Northwest Coastal Indians who used its bark for baskets, nets, rope, blankets, and clothing. Wood was used for canoes, dishes, ceremonial masks, posts, and totem poles. Split planks were used to build their houses.

DOUGLAS-FIR
Pseudotsuga menziesii
Pine Family   Up to 250 ft.

Douglas-fir is not a true fir (Abies), since its cone remains intact instead of falling apart. It is named for Archibald Menzies, the Scottish physician and naturalist who discovered the tree on Vancouver Island, B.C., in 1771. David Douglas, a Scottish botanist, sent seeds of the tree back to Europe in the 1820's; hence the common name Douglas-fir.

mpedersen

GRAND FIR
Abies grandis
Pine Family   Up to 250 ft.

Whimsy - This is the only true fir in the lowlands and is a favorite for Christmas trees. It has the sweet aroma of balsam. It is considered the most grand of all the firs in the lowlands, hence its name grandis.

NOBLE FIR
Abies procera
Pine Family   Up to 200 ft.

David Douglas named this tree because of its noble appearance. Old-growth noble firs are very impressive, with diameters up to 6 ft. and the first branch at 80 ft. or higher. In the forest environment, all the lower limbs die, leaving a tall straight tree.

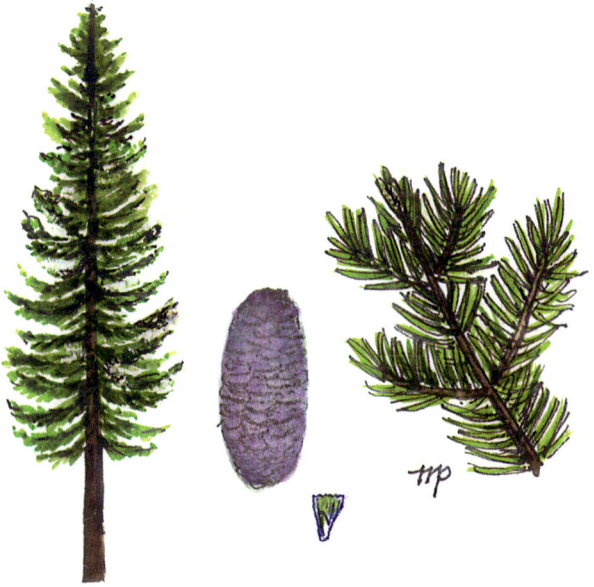

PACIFIC SILVER FIR
Abies amabilis
Pine Family   Up to 200 ft.

Most forest trees, including the Pacific silver fir, will develop an entirely different shape if grown in the open rather than in the forest. In the open, they will retain a Christmas tree shape, while in the forest setting they will have tall trunks with few if any lower branches.

Winter in the Cascade Mountains

npedersen

SUBALPINE FIR
Abies lasiocarpa
Pine Family   Up to 100 ft.

The tree form resembles the Eiffel Tower and makes a dramatic and eye-catching statement. Thickets which form at its base are used as cover for wildlife. Squirrels and mountain sheep eat the seeds.

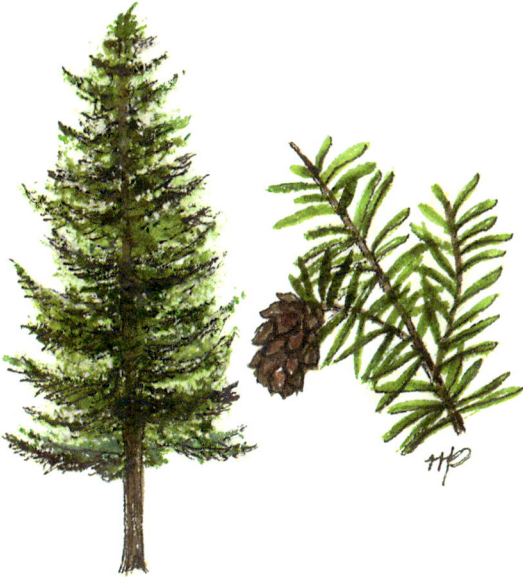

MOUNTAIN HEMLOCK
Tsuga mertensiana
Pine Family   Up to 100 ft.

This tree's usefulness is not restricted to commercial use but enhances our environment. They offer watershed protection, prevent erosion, provide clear, clean water and necessary habitat for birds and animals.

WESTERN HEMLOCK
Tsuga heterophylla
Pine Family   Up to 200 ft.

The Indians used the bark for roofing small houses
and drank tea made from the needles. The bark has
medicinal properties. Western hemlock's curled-over
top leader makes it easy to identify.

WESTERN JUNIPER
Juniperus occidentalis
Cypress Family   Up to 60 ft.

Long-lived, it survives in driest of areas and can affix itself to a rock peak. The Indians made bows of its wood and ate the berries.

WESTERN LARCH
Larix occidentalis
Pine Family   Up to 180 ft.

This is the only native conifer that is deciduous. The trees turn bright yellow in October, before the needles fall off. Western larch can live up to 500 years. The beautiful and distinctive grain of this wood and its workability with tools make it one of the great timber trees of the Northwest.

LODGEPOLE PINE
Pinus contorta
Pine Family   Up to 100 ft.

The Indians used poles made from the tall, straight
lodgepole pines for travois (sleds drawn by horses,
dogs or people), and for tepees, hence the name
lodgepole.

PONDEROSA PINE
Pinus ponderosa
Pine Family   Up to 200 ft.

Fire is part of the natural ecosystem of the ponderosa pine. A large pine can often withstand a forest fire which eliminates brush and small seedling trees and leaves an open, grassy, park-like stand of ponderosa to thrive.

**PONDEROSA PINE
CONE**

WESTERN WHITE PINE
Pinus monticola
Pine Family   Up to 130 ft.

This is the tree used for making matches and for wood carving because it is extremely soft and smooth and can be easily cut across the grain as well as with the grain. Blister rust, a fungus, kills many of these trees.

**WESTERN
WHITE PINE
CONE**

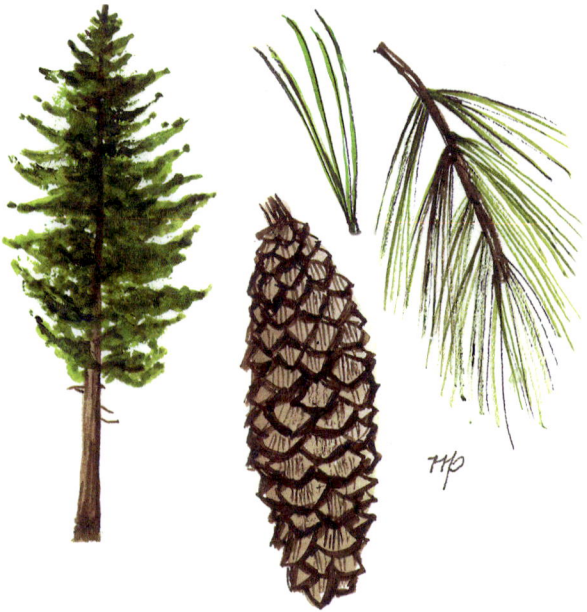

SUGAR PINE
Pinus lambertiana
Pine Family   Up to 200 ft.

David Douglas saw the large cones from this pine in an
Indian pouch and went off to see the tree that produced
the amazing cones. When he tried to shoot the cones
out of a tree, nearby Indians heard the shot and came to
investigate. He pacified them with tobacco. The sap is
very sweet, hence the name sugar pine.

REDWOOD
Sequoia sempervirens
Redwood Family   Up to 370 ft.

The Sequoia is named after the great Cherokee chief.
The specific name sempervirens means always green.
This tree normally lives 1000-1500 years.

SITKA SPRUCE
Picea sitchensis
Pine Family   Up to 200 ft.

A tea from the needles was of medicinal value to the
Indians and the resin was used as an ointment for
burns and wounds. The roots were woven into
clothing, fishing line, and baskets. The wood was also
used for small canoes. It has the highest strength-to-
weight ratio of any wood in the world. Pound for
pound it is stronger than steel.

PACIFIC YEW
Taxus brevifolia
Yew Family   Up to 35 ft.

Until recently the tree was considered a trash tree by
loggers and disposed of by burning. However,
although the berry is poisonous, it has recently been
discovered that the bark and needles yield taxol which
is valuable in some cancer therapy.

HPedersen

TREES
BROADLEAVES

RED ALDER
Alnus rubra
Birch Family   Up to 120 ft.

Red alder is important in the forest ecology because it adds nitrogen to the soil, a necessary process of our forest ecosystem. It was used by the Indians for smoking salmon, making kitchen utensils, and as a cure for indigestion.

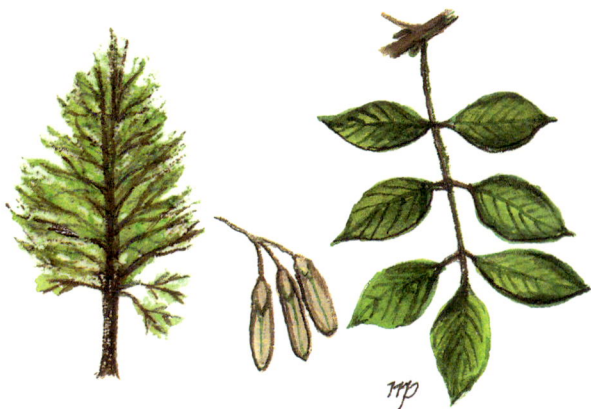

OREGON ASH
Fraxinus latifolia
Olive Family   Up to 80 ft.

Ash is called the sportsman's wood because of its strength. The rapidly-growing young tree produces wide growth rings which mean a stronger wood than one with narrow rings.

QUAKING ASPEN
Populus tremuloides
Willow Family   Up to 80 ft.

The leafstalk is flat, and so the leaf will tremble or flutter in the breeze, giving this tree the specific name tremuloides. Bears leave their claw marks and people leave their inscriptions which last for years on this bark. Beavers thrive on the inner bark and build their dams with aspen. Explorers and mountain men knew that where aspen grew, beaver and their pelts could be found.

A Farm on the Siletz River

CASCARA BUCKTHORN
Rhamnus purshiana
Buckthorn Family   Up to 50 ft.

"Cascara" means bark in Spanish. At one time, the entire world supply of bark used in making laxatives came from the Pacific Northwest; even if some bark is stripped from this tree, it will not die as long as a stump with some bark remains.

BLACK COTTONWOOD
Populus trichocarpa
Willow Family   Up to 200 ft.

Fast-growing, it is the largest member of the poplar
family in North America and the tallest broadleaf in
western North America. The pioneers found this tree
to be their only shade for hundreds of miles along
the trail.

Black Cottonwood

mpedersen

PACIFIC DOGWOOD

Cornus nuttallii
Dogwood Family   Up to 60 ft.

The name dogwood is derived from the dags or
skewers made from this tree - first called "dagwood"
then "dogwood." David Douglas first identified it as
the same tree as the eastern dogwood, but Thomas
Nuttall recognized it as a new species. This is
considered one of our most beautiful native trees.

PACIFIC MADRONE
Arbutus menziesii
Heath Family   Up to 100 ft.

In 1792 Archibald Menzies, the Scottish botanist, recognized and wrote of its singular beauty and value as an ornamental tree. The peeling bark makes it readily identifiable. Even in ample space this tree grows in a twisted manner.

Madrone Flower

BIG LEAF MAPLE
Acer macrophyllum
Maple Family   Up to 100 ft.

Maple sugar can be made from 50 gallons of sap
which boils down to 1 quart of syrup. The wonderful
large leaves enrich the soil and thus play a part in the
ecosystem.

VINE MAPLE

Acer circinatum
Maple Family   Up to 20 ft.

In the early days Indians made scoop nets out of its branches to catch salmon and the inner bark provided food to survive the long winter. Its brilliant fall colors make it a focal point in many Northwest gardens and in the wild.

OREGON MYRTLE
Umbellularia californica
Laurel Family   Up to 100 ft.

It is often called California laurel. Although neither a myrtle nor a laurel, it is in the laurel family. To overcome a chill, Hudson Bay Company trappers made a warming tea from the leaves of this tree. Its wood is highly prized, and products such as platters, bowls and trays are found in gift shops along the coast.

OREGON WHITE OAK

Quercus garryana
Beech Family   Up to 100 ft.

Leaves have as much protein as alfalfa hay and are
browsed by livestock and wild animals. Bears eat the
acorns. David Douglas reported that the Indians
soaked the acorns at the edge of streams and lakes in
the fall and ate them the following winter.

**TALL OAKS
FROM LITTLE ACORNS GROW**

DAVID EVERETT

SCOULER WILLOW
Salix scouleriana
Willow Family   Up to 50 ft.

This tree is called the fire willow because it springs up after forest fires. It was also given the name mountain willow because it can grow at elevations up to 10,000 ft.

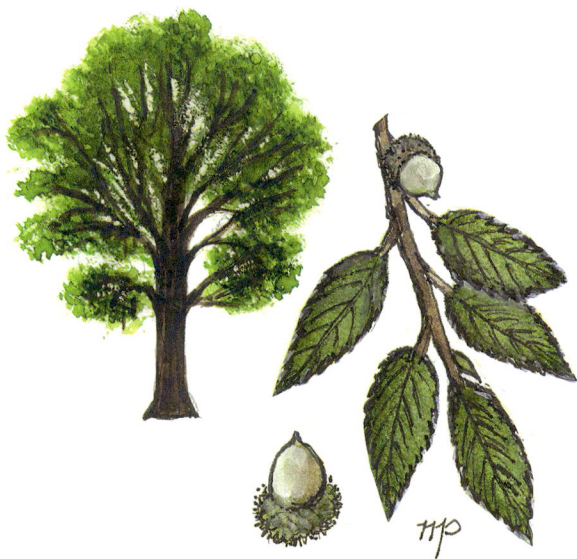

TANOAK
Lithocarpus densiflora
Beech Family   Up to 100 ft.

Historically the Native Americans ground the acorns
and cooked them for mush, soup, and bread. In the
winter they survived on this diet.

A Company Town on the Columbia

STUDYING TREES

A tree can be defined in the simplest terms as a tall, woody plant. Not all tall plants, however, are trees: for example, bamboo is tall, but it is a very tall grass, not a tree. Most trees have one trunk; but some may have two, three or more trunks. Some trees are more like shrubs or bushes. One thing is certain. All trees have wood and bark.

A tree sends down roots which can extend a long way from the trunk. The trunk is composed of three layers. Outside is a protective layer, the bark. Just inside the bark is a thin layer of living tissue, called the cambium, where water and nutrients travel up and down the trunk. Inside of this living layer is the non-living core or wood of the tree which provides strong support for the leafy tree top called the crown.

Trees of the Northwest can be classified into two categories: conifers and broadleaf trees. Conifers produce seeds in cones. Cone-producing trees include such trees as firs and pines and are sometimes called "softwoods" because their wood is usually soft and

easy to saw and shape. The thin leaves on conifers are called "needles." The needles may be short as they are on firs or long as they are on most pines. Most conifers are evergreen, retaining their needles all year long. A few, however, such as the larch are deciduous and lose their needles in winter. Cone-bearing trees are much more ancient than flowering trees like magnolias. Their ancestors lived during the age of the dinosaurs. Flowering trees came much later, coinciding with the spread of mammals over the earth. The broadleaves are sometimes called "hardwoods" because the wood is often very hard and dense. Broadleaves include such trees as maples, oaks, alders, and cottonwoods. Most broadleaf trees are deciduous, meaning they lose their leaves in winter.

Individual trees can live to be hundreds of years old. Each year a tree grows it adds new growth around the trunk. Each year of growth can be seen as a "ring" when the tree is cut down. By counting the rings we can learn how old a tree is.

– Linda McMahan

Mt. Hood Oregon

HABITATS

WETLANDS

HABITATS

ALPINE WOODLANDS

TREE-SONG

*T*hrough lines of aspens and alders
A sudden, warm wind sings
Its ancient, summer tree-song,
And conducts their branches in
An adagio for strings.

The panoply of leaves
In shadow-patterned sunlight
Displays its summer's lushness -
Boasts of abundant life.
But soon through black, bare branches
The wind, now touched with ice,
In its endless ambiguity
Has become the winter's knife.

– Don Cosart

LATIN WORDS USED IN PLANT NAMES

amabilis - pretty
brevifolia - short foliage
californica - found in California
circinatum - coiled
contorta - twisted
decurrens - leaf base that merges with the stem
densiflora - densely-flowered
garryana - named for Nicholas Garry, assistant to David
       Douglas
grandis - big or showy
heterophylla - diversely-leaved
lambertiana - named for Aylmer Lambert, English botanist
lasiocarpa - woolly-fruited
latifolia - wide-leaved
macrophyllum - big-leaved
menziesii - named for Archibald Menzies, Scottish botanist
mertensiana - named for Franz Carl Mertens, German
       botanist
monticola - mountain-dwelling
nuttallii - named for Thomas Nuttall, English botanist
occidentalis - western
plicata - pleated
ponderosa - heavy
procera - tall
purshiana - named for Frederick Pursh, German explorer
       and collector
rubra - red
scouleriana - named for John Scouler, Scottish naturalist
sempervirens - always green
sitchensis - from Sitka, Alaska
tremuloides - trembling or quivering
trichocarpa - hairy-fruited

NAME	LEAVES	FRUIT
RED ALDER	3-4 in. long, egg-shaped with double-toothed edges, deciduous.	Cones are small, up to 1 in. long, brown, and woody.
OREGON ASH	Up to 14 in. long, comprised of 5-9 leaflets oppositely arranged on the leafstalk, deciduous.	Winged seeds shaped like canoes, called samaras, hanging in clusters.
QUAKING ASPEN	2-3 in. wide, heart-shaped, with slightly saw-toothed edges. Bright yellow fall foliage, deciduous.	Tiny cone-shaped capsules with cottony seeds.
CASCARA BUCKTHORN	2-5 in. long, shiny and prominently veined, deciduous.	Little red fruits which turn black late in the season, inedible to humans, but loved by birds.
BLACK COTTONWOOD	3-6 in. long, green above and silvery white below, deciduous.	Capsules are attached to a drooping spike. Inside fruit are tiny, cottony seeds which act like parachutes and can be carried for miles by the wind.
PACIFIC DOGWOOD	4-5 in. long, upper surface bright green with pronounced veins, deciduous.	Red berries in small clusters. Flowers comprised of yellow-green florets surrounded by 4-6 large white bracts.

BARK	HABITAT	USES
Gray-white with black patches. May also have white lichen patches. Inner bark turns red when exposed to the air, hence the specific name rubra.	Most common broadleaf in western Oregon, especially found beside streams.	Its rapid growth and wide range make it our most important broadleaf. Large logs are used for cabinets, furniture, paper pulp, and firewood.
Dark gray or brown.	Abundant in western Oregon and Washington. Likes moisture of sloughs, streambanks, and lowlands.	Fuel, tool handles, furniture, baseball bats, and barrels.
Smooth and white.	Grows sparingly in Oregon and Washington mostly in the Cascades and eastward.	Shredding qualities make it useful for packing and wallboard. Rarely used for lumber.
Thin, gray and splotchy.	Northwest forests from coast to Cascades. Grows in deep, moist shade as an understory tree.	Historically the bark was used for laxatives and as a tonic. Wood not commercially desirable.
Pale gray and furrowed or ridged on mature trees.	Rivers and streams throughout most of Oregon and Washington.	Extensively used for paper pulp and boxes. Wood is soft and weak, not useful for many timber products.
Thin, gray, and smooth.	West of the Cascades in mixed forests.	A beautiful native tree. Birds, largely finches, pigeons, and thrushes, eat the berries. Indians used bark extract instead of quinine with good results.

NAME	LEAVES	FRUIT
DOUGLAS-FIR	Needles 1 in. long, dark to pale green, arranged around twigs in bottle-brush style.	Cones 3-4 in. long, brown. Conspicuous three-pointed bracts extend beyond cone scales, resembling a mouse's hind legs and tail sticking out of a hole. Cones droop from ends of the branches.
GRAND FIR	Needles 1 ½-2 in. long, flat, shiny, dark green above, white below in a flat spray.	Cone 2 ½-4 ¼ in. long, green. Erect clusters of cones on most branches, especially near the top of the tree, disintegrate at maturity.
NOBLE FIR	Needles, bluish-green, bent upwards to a form resembling hockey sticks.	Cones 4-6 in. long, erect, purple to brown, having conspicuous bracts with downward pointed ends, mostly on upper branches, disintegrate at maturity.
PACIFIC SILVER FIR	Needles about 1 ¼ in. long, shiny green on top and silver beneath, in flattened, spray-like branches.	Cones 3-6 in. long, deep purple, upright on the upper branches, like all true firs (Abies), disintegrate at maturity.
SUBALPINE FIR	Needles are 1-2 in. long and appear to be brushed upward.	Cones, up to 4 in. long, purple, grow straight upward on the upper branches, looking like little owls, and completely fall apart at maturity.
MOUNTAIN HEMLOCK	Needles under 1 in. long, blue green, star-like on short stalks.	Cones 1-3 in. long, usually purple, drooping from the branches.

BARK	HABITAT	USES
Smooth, gray with resin blisters in young trees. In old-growth trees it is thick and deeply furrowed. The thick bark enables the Douglas-fir to survive forest fires and then reseed burned areas.	From the coast to the Cascades and in the mountains of eastern Oregon. It adapts to a variety of soils, best on moist, well-drained soils. Forms pure or nearly pure stands.	Provides high-grade, general-purpose lumber. Made into more products for human use than any other tree - houses, poles, beams, paper, boats, etc. Douglas-fir forests are important habitat for a wide diversity of wildlife including spotted owls, flying squirrels, pine martens, pileated woodpeckers and many other species. Christmas trees are exported worldwide.
Gray to light brown.	Both east and west of the Cascades. Mingles with other conifers in mixed stands.	Limited use of this softwood in boxes and paper goods, also for Christmas trees.
Purple-gray in young trees and red-brown in mature trees.	3,000-7,000 ft. in the Cascade range in Oregon and Washington. This tree is resistant to insect damage.	Used for interior finishing, doors, and windows. It is a popular Christmas tree.
Older bark gray to nearly white, usually smooth, often with pitch pockets or resin blisters.	Mid to high elevations of the Cascades from Crater Lake northward.	Wood is pale yellow, soft and light, and not particularly good for lumber but is used in crates, boxes and for paper pulp. Silver fir forests are important for watershed protection and wildlife habitat.
Thin, grey and smooth.	Generally 4,000 to 8,000 ft. in the Blue, Cascade and Olympic Mountains.	The wood is too soft for timber products. Subalpine fir's beauty is particularly appreciated by photographers.
Purplish or reddish-brown, cracked and furrowed.	Mountains, subalpine to timberline (4,000-7,000 ft.), generally above the range of the western hemlock.	Its soft, light wood is not valuable for lumber but can be used for pulp.

NAME	LEAVES	FRUIT
WESTERN HEMLOCK	Needles rather short, from $\frac{1}{4}$ to $\frac{3}{4}$ in. long, flat along the side of the twig in two rows.	Cones 1 in. or smaller, egg-shaped, thin with smooth scales.
INCENSE-CEDAR	$\frac{1}{8}$ in. long. Each segment on the stem includes four scale-like leaves. Fragrant when crushed.	Cones $\frac{3}{4}$ in. long, shaped like a duck's bill.
WESTERN JUNIPER	Needles $\frac{1}{8}$ in. long, grey-green and scale-like, scratchy to touch.	Blue berries up to $\frac{1}{3}$ in. in diameter, each containing 2-3 seeds.
WESTERN LARCH	Needles 1-1 $\frac{3}{4}$ in. long, clustered in bundles of 14-30, on stout woody pegs, bright yellow fall foliage color, deciduous.	Cones small and woody 1-2 in. long, termed "whiskery" because of long-tipped bracts.
PACIFIC MADRONE	3-5 in. long, glossy green above and whitish underneath, evergreen.	Cluster of pea-sized bright red and orange berries. Flowers are clustered spikes of white jug-shaped blooms on tiny stalks.
BIG LEAF MAPLE	6-12 in. across (largest of all maples), with five main lobes resembling a hand. Brilliant yellow fall foliage, deciduous.	Double-winged seeds (samaras) form a "V", adapted for air travel.
VINE MAPLE	3-4 in. long with 5-9 lobes having serrated edges. Fall color bright gold or blazing red, deciduous.	Double samaras (thin, winged seeds) 1 $\frac{1}{2}$ in. long, red or rose in color.

BARK	HABITAT	USES
Cinnamon brown with flattened ridges, about 1 in. thick.	From the coast to the crest of the Cascades. Shade tolerant, a western hemlock can grow to maturity in a generally shady environment. This is the dominant tree in the climax forest west of the Cascades.	High quality pulp used for newsprint, magazines, tissue paper. Wood used for flooring.
Dark brown and furrowed.	Mostly southern Oregon Cascades in mixed stands of trees.	Wood is used for pencils because it is soft and will not splinter when machined. Also used for fence posts and cedar chests.
Cinnamon brown in scaly plates, shreddy.	Northeast and central Oregon and southeast Washington. Often found in pure stands.	Durable wood which is ideal for long-lasting fence posts. Also used as firewood.
Reddish-orange, furrowed and 3-6 in. thick at maturity.	In the Cascades and eastward in both Washington and Oregon.	Used in construction and interior finish of homes and in furniture.
Reddish-brown and smooth, constantly peeling.	West side of the Cascades from British Columbia to California.	Limited commercial use for timber products because of warping and checking. Used for firewood.
Brown to red-brown, often covered with green moss and ferns.	In and west of the Cascades in open country and conifer forests.	An important hardwood for furniture, interior finish, flooring and boat building.
Smooth.	West of the Cascades, in damp soil. This small tree grows under conifers and also in open rocky areas.	Foliage is browsed by deer and elk, and squirrels and birds eat the seeds.

NAME	LEAVES	FRUIT
OREGON MYRTLE	2-6 in. long, 1 in. wide, shiny, with a pungent camphor-like odor when crushed, evergreen.	Olive-like in clusters, pale yellow-green when ripe.
OREGON WHITE OAK	3-6 in. long with 7-9 rounded lobes, shiny green, deciduous.	An acorn 1 in. long with a cap.
LODGEPOLE PINE	Needles 1-3 in. long (shortest of all the pines), in bundles of two.	Smallest pine cone, 1-2 in. long, egg-shaped.
PONDEROSA PINE	Needles 5-10 in. long, rich yellow-green in bundles of three.	Cones 3-6 in. long, scales ending in a prickly tip.
SUGAR PINE	Needles 1 $\frac{1}{2}$-4 in. long in bundles of five. Whitish on all three surfaces.	Cones 10-20 in. long, fat and woody. Longest cone in the world.
WESTERN WHITE PINE	Needles 2-4 in. long in bundles of five. Soft, fine, blue-green with a frosty appearance.	Cones 5-18 in. long, curved and slender. After seeds release the mature cone falls to the ground, as with all pines.
WESTERN REDCEDAR	Needles $\frac{1}{8}$-$\frac{1}{4}$ in. long that are scale-like and interwoven, arranged in flat sprays, shiny yellow-green above.	Upright cones $\frac{1}{2}$ in. long, found on female tree, shaped like tiny rosebuds.

BARK	HABITAT	USES
Thin and scaly when mature.	Close to water, along stream bottoms in southwestern Oregon and into California.	Highest priced of western hardwoods, it polishes like marble with a beautiful grain when finished. Great commercial value for furniture, cabinets, and curios.
Gray, shaggy, shallowly ridged.	Interior valleys of western Oregon and Washington and in the Columbia Gorge. Oak does best in open, sunny areas. Slow growing.	Good for floors, furniture, and shipbuilding, but eastern supplies of white oak are more abundant, so Oregon white oak is little used.
Very thin ($\frac{1}{4}$ in.), dark and flaky.	Inland at 3,000-9,000 ft. in the Cascade and Blue Mountains where the trees grows tall and straight. Also found at the coast where the tree is shortened and bent by the winds.	Used for composition board, poles, posts, and fiber products.
On mature or old-growth trees the color is bright orange to yellow. Flakes off like a puzzle piece.	Most widely distributed pine in North America. Most common in Oregon and Washington east of the Cascades and in southern Oregon.	Second only to Douglas-fir in commercial importance, it is used in many phases of residential construction. Important for watershed protection and wildlife habitat east of the Cascades.
Red-brown and furrowed.	Southern Oregon Cascades and occasionally as far north as the Mt. Hood National Forest.	Highly valued softwood. Used for such products as shakes and moldings.
Silver-gray, small squares resembling bathroom tile.	Mountainous areas of the Northwest in mixed forests.	Used for interior trim, paneling, cabinets, and picture frames because it doesn't warp or shrink.
Reddish-brown, thin, will peel off in long strips.	Occurs from the coast to the Cascade Mountains along creeks, but usually not found in pure stands.	Resistant to decay, it is primarily used for shingles and shakes, boats, and posts.

NAME	LEAVES	FRUIT
REDWOOD	Needles ½-1 in. long, shiny, in a flat spray.	Cones ¾-1 in. long, woody.
SITKA SPRUCE	Needles 1 in. long, extending from all sides of the stem, very prickly.	Cones up to 4 in. long, pale-yellow to tan, hanging down from the branches.
TANOAK	3-5 in. long, simple, dentate, and prominently veined, evergreen.	Acorn with a spiny cap. Flower is a long erect spike of white flowers like candles at Christmas.
SCOULER WILLOW	2-4 in. long, yellow-green, deciduous.	1/3 in. long seed capsule appearing late in growing season. Flower, appearing in spring, is an erect cylindrical catkin.
PACIFIC YEW	Needles ½-1 in. long, dark green above and light green below. Only conifer with an all-green needle.	Small coral-red berries with a single large seed.

BARK	HABITAT	USES
Red-brown, coarsely fibrous, up to 12 in. thick in older trees.	Primarily in the fogbelt of northern California, but extending up into extreme southern Oregon along the coast.	One of the world's most versatile woods, it is immune to termites, durable, soft and workable, but not suitable for structural uses. Used commonly for posts, columns, decking, siding, paneling, doors and shingles. Unfortunately, redwood forests are becoming increasingly rare.
Thin, gray-brown, scaly.	Coastal areas from Alaska to northern California and up to 3,000 ft. in elevation.	Excellent for various products like garage doors, doors, ladders and musical instruments such as violins and pianos.
Dark gray with high tannin content.	Grows from sea level to 5,000 ft. Follows the redwood from southern Oregon to northern California.	At one time Native Americans used the tannin to tan leather. Has limited commercial use for plywood, flooring, furniture, and paper.
Dull gray with bitter but harmless quinine taste.	Abundant in the Northwest along streams.	No commercial value but reduces stream bank erosion. Wild animals, especially beaver, eat the twigs, bark and flowers. Historically, Indians wove baskets of willow twigs.
Rusty-red, thin, papery, and peeling.	Always an understory tree, growing in the shady moist forests of the Northwest from the Cascades to the coast, especially along streams.	Heavy tough wood good for bows, canoe paddles, and things that require resilience.

FRUITS, SEEDS AND FLOWERS

Acorns

Double key maples

samaras

Cones

Berries

FLOWERS

64

LEAF STRUCTURES AND ARRANGEMENTS

SIMPLE

LANCE

HEART

TOOTHED

OVAL

ALTERNATE

LOBED

NEEDLES

OPPOSITE

QUIZ
NAME THESE LEAVES

1. _____ 2. _____ 3. _____

NAMES THESE FRUITS

1. _____ 2. _____ 3. _____ 4. _____

Fruit Answers:
1. Red Alder
2. Oregon White Oak
3. Pacific Silver Fir
4. Vine Maple

Leaf Answers:
1. Madrone
2. Vine Maple
3. Quaking Aspen

GLOSSARY

Acorn - a seed of the oak tree.

Alpine - in the vicinity of timberline.

Bract - small leaf-like structure.

Cambium - the layer just under the bark, it is the actively growing part of the trunk.

Canopy - the layer of branches of the tallest trees in the forest.

Catkin - compact spike of flowers.

Compound - a leaf made up of several leaflets.

Cone - a woody mass of seeds and scales.

Conifer - cone-bearing tree.

Crown - the upper part of a tree.

Deciduous - trees that drop all of their leaves in the fall.

Dendrologist - a person who studies leaves of trees.

Dentate - toothed margin.

Ecology - the science of the relationship of plants, animals, and the environment.

Ecosystem - naturally occurring association of plants and animals in a given environment.

Evergreen - bearing green leaves throughout the year.

Family - the biological classification between order and genus, usually includes several genera. Example: the Pine family includes the genera- Abies, Cedrus, Larix, Picea, Pinus, et. al.

Flower - part of the plant containing the reproductive organs.

Fruit - part of the plant which bears the seeds.

Furrowed - having long and shallow grooves.

Genus - the biological classification between family and species. The first of a plant's two botanical names.

Habitat - the nature of the environment in which a plant or animal lives.

Hardwood - broadleaf tree.

Heartwood - inactive, old wood at the center of the tree trunk.

Leaf - the usually flat outgrowth from the stem where food is manufactured, includes needles.

Leaflet - a single part of a compound leaf.

Lichen - an association of fungi and algae growing together on a solid surface such as a tree branch.

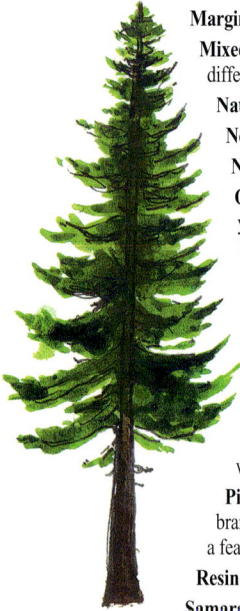

Lobe - a rounded segment of an organ, often a leaf.

Margin - the edge of a leaf.

Mixed Conifer Forest - forest in which several different conifer species grow. (Mixed stand).

Native - grows naturally in a particular place.

Needles - leaves that are long and thin.

Nut - one form of fruit.

Old-growth Forest - predominantly trees 250 years old or older with an abundance of down logs and standing dead trees.

Opposite - reference to leaves which grow in pairs directly opposite each other along the stem.

Palmate - having three or more veins, lobes, or leaflets radiating from a single point like the fingers of a hand.

Photosynthesis - plant process for manufacturing starch or cellulose from sunlight, water, carbon dioxide and chlorophyll.

Pinnate - having plant parts (veins, lobes, branches) arranged on opposite sides of an axis, like a feather.

Resin - pitch.

Samara - a winged fruit.

Sapling - a young tree.

Scale - a small leaf-like covering of a bud, thick flat structures of a cone, and flakes of bark.

Seedling - very young plant.

Serrate - saw-toothed, with teeth pointing forward toward the point of the leaf.

Shrub - a woody plant with many branching stalks.

Simple - a leaf with only one blade.

Snag - standing dead tree.

Softwood - conifer.

Species - the biological classification below genus, forms the second part of the Latin botanical–name of a plant.

Stand - a group of trees.

Stomata - cells in the skin on the underside of a leaf or stem which permit the exchange of gases between the plant and the atmosphere.

Timberline - the uppermost elevation on a mountain at which trees can grow.

Veins - the rib-like channels which carry the sap through the leaf.

Watershed - all the land which drains into a particular stream.

CONSERVATION AND PRESERVATION
TREES AND THE QUALITY OF LIFE

Trees play an important role in our lives. Environmentally, they absorb carbon dioxide, emit oxygen from their leaves, and absorb water through their roots thereby deterring erosion and flooding. Trees provide habitat and often food for birds, insects, and small animals. Trees furnish fuel, lumber, and paper; and some trees provide food and medicines for human consumption. When leaves fall and when trees die, they decompose and return nutrients and minerals to the soil as fertilizer for other plant growth.

Trees provide shade, circulate air, act as a noise barrier, and soften the visual impact of development with their greenery and structural forms. Trees give us a sense of seasons, and in doing so, add color to our lives.

In many communities, trees are disappearing faster than they are being replanted. Just imagine what your neighborhood would be like without trees.

SELECTED BIBLIOGRAPHY

Bowers, Nathan A., *Cone-Bearing Trees of the Pacific Coast.* Palo Alto, California: Pacific Books, McGraw H. Hill Book Co., 1965.

Brockman, C. Frank & Rebecca Merrilees, *A Guide to Field Identification of Trees of North America.* New York: Golden Press, Western Publishing Company, Inc. 1979.

Eliot, Willard Ayres, *Forest Trees of the Pacific Coast.* New York: G.P. Putnam's Sons, 1938.

Jensen, Edward C. & Charles R. Ross, *Trees to Know in Oregon.* Oregon State University Extension Service and Oregon Department of Forestry, 1994.

Little, Elbert L., *The Audubon Society Field Guide to North American Trees.* New York: Alfred A. Knopf, 1980.

Peattie, Donald Culross, *A Natural History of Western Trees.* Boston: Houghton Mifflin Company, 1953.

Petrides, George A. & Olivia Petrides, *A Field Guide to Western Trees, The Peterson Field Guide Series.* Boston-New York: Houghton Mifflin Company, 1992.

Preston, Jr., Richard J., *North American Trees.* Cambridge, Massachusetts: M.I.T. Press, 1978.

Russo, Monica, *The Tree Almanac.* New York: Sterling Publishing Company, Inc., 1993.

Sudworth, George B., *Forest Trees of the Pacific Slope.* New York: Dover Publications, Inc., 1967.

Taylor, Ronald J. & George W. Douglas, *Mountain Plants of the Pacific Northwest.* Missoula, Montana: Mountain Press Publication Company, 1995.

Whitney, Stephen, *Audubon Society's Nature Guide to Western Forests.* New York: Alfred Knopf. 1985.

Wiedemann, Alfred M. (Prepared by), *Your Tour Guide to the Plants of Salishan.* Salishan Lodge, Gleneden Beach, Oregon, 1972.

INDEX

CONTRIBUTORS

This work was made possible by members of The Portland Garden Club and the Katherine Pamplin Educational Endowment Fund.

Concept and Illustrations - Martha Pedersen

Editor - Carolyn Cosart

Calligrapher - Janet Charlton

Botanical Consultants - Russ Jolley, Botanical Consultant, and Linda McMahan, Executive Director, Berry Botanic Garden

Jeanne Becker	Geraldine Fettig
Elizabeth Brooke	Jean Grelle
Sue Brownell	Kay Hill
Susan Cooley	Sara Mauritz
Don Cosart	Maxine Sims
Dede DeJager	Sister Patricia Stebinger
Mary Ericksen	

Object of The Portland Garden Club
"To stimulate the knowledge and love of gardening, to aid in the protection of native trees, plants and birds, to encourage civic beauty, and to improve and protect the quality of the environment through programs and action in the fields of conservation and education."